Made in the USA
Monee, IL
07 March 2022

92433278R00062